Healing from Within

A Chakra and Ho'oponopono Healing Guidebook

Wendi M. Lindenmuth B.S, MPH

Healing from Within

A Chakra and Ho'oponopono Healing Guidebook.

All Rights Reserved

No part of this book may be used or reproduced in any manner without the author's written permission, except for brief quotations used in reviews and critiques. Contact for Use Permissions: wenlinden@live.com. This book is not a substitute for licensed physicians or mental health practitioners' medical or mental health advice. The reader should regularly consult a physician in matters relating to his/her health, particularly concerning any symptoms requiring diagnosis or medical attention.

Lora and Ariel fonts were used with permission from Microsoft.

COPYRIGHT © 2021 Wendi M. Lindenmuth

ISBN: 978-0-578-84766-5

Cover design by DC Cover Creations

Chakra illustrations by Wendi M. Lindenmuth

Edited by Piers Knightingale and Michelle Guajardo

Published by Healing Forward

Other Titles by Wendi M. Lindenmuth

Dear Lyme Disease: Transforming Your Pain into Purpose

Dedication

To my mom, Nancy, who encourages me to do and be my best every day.

Contents

Dedication..5
Introduction..9
Understanding Your Chakras...................................19
Understanding Ho'oponopono.................................25
Root Chakra..33
Sacral Chakra..47
Solar Plexus Chakra..61
Heart Chakra..75
Throat Chakra..89
Third Eye Chakra...103
Crown Chakra..117
Using All of Your Chakras......................................129
Conclusion..132
Resources..135
Appendix A...137
Acknowledgments..173

Mission Statement & Disclaimer

All information obtained from the author of this book, Wendi M. Lindenmuth, is to be taken solely as advisory in nature. Wendi does not dispense medical or other professional advice or prescribe the use of any technique as a form of diagnosis or treatment for any physical, emotional, or mental conditions.

The author's intent is only to offer information of an anecdotal and general nature that may be part of your quest for emotional and spiritual well-being. Suppose you or others use the information or contents of this book. In that case, the author assumes no responsibility for the direct or indirect consequences and will not be held personally, legally, or financially liable for any action taken based upon her advice.

The reader should consult his/her medical, health, or other professional before using any of the book's suggestions or drawing inferences from it. The reader acknowledges that he/she/assumes full responsibility for the knowledge gained and how they utilize and exercise the information in this book and its application. Anyone using the information in this book acknowledges that they have read and understood this disclaimer's details.

Introduction

Life has a funny way of guiding you in a direction that you would have never taken unless something significant happened in your life. That happened to me when I became very ill and discovered chakras, Ho'oponopono, and journaling.

In my book, Dear Lyme Disease, I share my healing journey from when I was diagnosed with Lyme Disease, my progress, and where I am today. I think it is worth sharing again to understand the significance of how this book came about and the power of the information it contains.

In 2015, I became extremely ill with chronic Lyme Disease and other life-threatening illnesses and symptoms. It altered every aspect of my life, finances, relationships, health, spirituality, and purpose. Before I became ill, being physically active as a competitive athlete, and staying busy, consumed my life. I never had time to focus on my spirituality. After my diagnosis, I found myself bedridden for almost a year, unable to function mentally and physically. I could feel my soul crying out; finally, it had my full attention.

My soul was seeking something more fulfilling. It was calling out to feel whole once again, to awaken from its slumber. At first, I tried to ignore the messages and nudges that my soul was giving me. It felt uncomfortable and too foreign to make sense of living a new way of life.

Finally, after months of being stubborn, I gave into an inner voice that called to me and told me I had a second chance to do things differently. Ready or not, I found the faith to take the first step and began asking questions, searching for new answers, and gaining a new perspective on life. I was on my way to a new spiritual journey and discovering a new purpose in life.

I continued to search for answers while I recovered from my illness and symptoms. Ultimately, I was looking for alternative healing tools to use for myself and at home to improve my life quality and feel like I had some control.

I was eager to investigate alternative and spiritual healing methods besides Western Medicine that could benefit me. I did not have anything to lose. Although traditional medicine did play an essential role in my healing, I often felt I had little or no control over my health. I was still physically, mentally, emotionally, and spiritually ill and not improving. I needed more than waiting and hoping for the next medical protocol or medicine to start feeling better. It was also essential to learn something that was not overwhelming to use or too complicated.

As I searched for healing modalities that fit my criteria, I discovered Chakras and Ho'oponopono. They were both straightforward yet powerful healing modalities that have been around since ancient times. I learned and implemented chakras and Ho'oponopono into my daily life and was amazed at how my entire life began to change.

By combining these two healing practices, I utilized their incredible healing energy and accelerated my healing. My inner self and my outlook on life started changing. I became stronger, healthier, and more attuned with Mother Earth, the Universe, and God.

As I continued to learn, I began to understand what science already had proven. Everything in the Universe has a frequency and rate at which it vibrates. All the different vibrations are continually responding and integrating with other frequencies like a beautiful, graceful dance.

You and I are continuously vibrating at different speeds, attracting and repelling similar frequencies. Working with chakras and Ho'oponopono will help you increase your vibration at a much higher frequency. It will also help heal and solve challenges in your life and your health.

I hope to teach you how to use chakras and Ho'oponopono in your daily life, to witness the magic of this healing, and find the answers you have been searching for.

Why This Book is for You

I created this guidebook with you in mind. It will show you how to connect your body, mind, and spirit at a deeper level by using chakras, the ancient Hawaiian practice of Ho'oponopono and journaling. When you implement these tools into your daily life, you will accelerate your emotional, physical, mental, and spiritual growth and healing.

As with anything, the more you practice, the more you learn how to be fully present and embody your whole self, inside and out. You will learn to experience joy, peace, fulfillment, freedom, forgiveness, gratitude, love, and real transformation.

Within this book, you will:

- Learn how to become and feel fully aligned and balanced in your life
- Understand the importance of the chakra system and how it works
- Learn about individual chakras each week and how they affect your emotional, spiritual, mental, and physical well-being
- Learn that what you feel within yourself mirrors how you think about life
- Learn the concepts of Ho'oponopono (Forgive me, I am sorry, I love you, Thank you), ancient Hawaiian art of living
- Learn how to change your beliefs and energy to start feeling better emotionally, physically, mentally, and spiritually
- Learn how to use the power of your chakras and Ho'oponopono together to support your healing and live a happier, healthier life
- Learn how to integrate journaling as a healing component in your life.

How to Read This Book

You will find this book easy to follow, learn, and do each chapter's assignments for seven weeks. You will start by understanding what chakras and Ho'oponopono are before you jump into learning about each chakra.

You will first learn about your chakra energy system, starting with the root, sacral, solar plexus, heart, throat, third eye, and crown chakras. Each chapter follows the same layout. You will learn each chakra's location in your body, the area of the body involved, their characteristics, focus and meaning, and how it feels when your chakras are out of alignment. You will also learn ways to nourish your chakras and how old you are when each chakra develops. You will have an assignment, self-assessment journaling questions, a Ho'oponopono activity, and a meditation.

While you focus on each chakra for a week, you may add a full chakra meditation a few times a week to work on all your chakras and get them flowing and working correctly. You can find the full chakra meditation in Chapter 10. There is no right or wrong way to work on your chakras. I have found that many beginners want to focus and learn about each chakra first. You can choose to apply the full chakra meditation when you feel comfortable.

Journaling is an essential aspect of this book. By incorporating journaling and Ho'oponopono with chakras, you will begin experiencing positive shifts in your emotional, physical, mental, and spiritual health and life.

There is ample space to write the answers and take notes in the book or use your favorite journal or notebook if you choose. But please actually do the assignments and write out your answers to the journal questions. Why is this important?

The simple act of journaling is incredibly beneficial for your mind, body, and spirit. Journaling is a great tool that allows you the space to get your thoughts out of your head and on paper and reset. It can also help with:

- Reducing stress
- Managing depression
- Reducing anxiety
- Calming your fears
- Providing an opportunity to practice positive encouragement and self-talk
- Speeding up a physical, emotional, mental, and spiritual healing
- Improving your mood
- Increasing feelings of well-being
- Improving your memory
- Increasing your awareness and insight

With the combination of chakras, Ho'oponopono, and journaling, you are on your way to exciting and profound changes in your life. But you must do the work. You cannot just read through the book, not do the assignments, and expect your life situations to change. Showing up and doing the work is essential to your growth and healing.

If at any time the information feels overwhelming or you are tired, take a break and rest, and then revisit it when your mind is fresh. I know when I read something new, I get excited and want to jump in headfirst. Then, I realize I need to step back a bit. Allow time to digest the information and then return to it when it feels right, and you are ready.

Now, find a comfortable and quiet place to read and write. Get ready to learn, do the work required, and start positively transforming your life by understanding your chakra energy system.

Chakra Energy System

Chapter 1
Understanding Your Chakras

This first chapter will help you become familiar with chakras. If you are already familiar with chakras, this is an excellent review and an opportunity to learn something new.

The Sanskrit word Chakra translates to a wheel or disk. In yoga, meditation, and Ayurveda, this term refers to wheels of energy throughout the body. Within each of our bodies, we have an incredible energy system consisting of multiple chakras. They each play a vital role in every aspect of our lives, including our health, career, and relationships. These chakras also govern our lives' different areas (emotional, physical, spiritual, and mental).

This book will teach you about the seven main chakras: root, sacral, solar plexus, heart, throat, third eye, and crown. Your chakras start from the base of your spine and extend through the top of your head.

When you visualize a chakra in your body, imagine a swirling wheel of energy where matter and consciousness meet. This invisible healing energy, called Prana, is a vital life force, which keeps us vibrant, healthy, and alive. If you cannot visualize a spinning wheel of energy within your body, that is ok. The important thing is to focus on the specific area of your body and each chakra's location. You can also put your hand on the chakra you are working on to focus better and not worry about imagining it spinning. Your intention is what matters the most, and the healing will still work.

Imagine your chakras as little self-generators, regulating and continuing to sustain certain aspects of your life and health. They each have a specific task. When one is not working properly, it impacts the others. Each chakra is an integral part of an energetic system supporting your physical body. They are conduits that conduct and transform energy into material form. Proper and unrestricted energy flow through your chakras is necessary for physical, mental, and good emotional health.

Balancing your chakras helps you to restore and enhance your energy flow. Chakras are centers of radiant power within your subtle (energetic) body, representing the dynamic intersection between physical matter and consciousness. If your chakras are not functioning correctly, the associated organs and systems in your body become impaired.

The Benefits of Working with the Chakras

Learning to work with your chakras will help you discover

innovative ways to see and feel your inner self and your life in a whole new way. It will show you new insights to have healthier behavior patterns and a more rewarding lifestyle. Your chakras will connect you more thoroughly with other people and experience inner peace. Each chakra is a window that opens to a higher energetic, psychic, and spiritual knowledge. Or it can remain closed, restricting you to your present limitations.

When your energy is flowing smoothly through each chakra and between the chakras, you tend to be:

- More positive
- Look better and feel better
- More self-confident and self-assured
- Communicate your thoughts, hopes, and dreams more healthily
- More balanced and be more focused
- More resilient and increased natural immunity
- Deal better with stress
- More intuitive and you will have a clearer insight into your purpose in the world.

Chakra work involves a simple yet powerful technique that can help you develop inner poise and balance your life. This practice is most helpful when you reinforce it daily with regular self-analysis and doing inner work. Working on your chakras is an adventure of self-discovery. I am excited for you to start your journey!

When to work with chakra energy

Everyday traumas and challenges can cause your energy to become blocked and stagnant. If you feel disconnected from yourself and the world around you, this is the perfect time to work on your lower chakras. If your life feels dull and needs more inspiration, working with your higher chakras will bring significant changes in your life and be more in line with your spiritual goals.

Why Chakras Don't Work Properly

Just like you, your chakras become tired, ill, and malnourished, and then they cannot do their job correctly. There are many influences on our chakras, causing them not to work correctly, such as pain, darkness, and memories in your life. Not consciously working on them will cause unbalance too. When you heal your chakras (energy system), your experiences and circumstances profoundly change.

Chakra Cleansing and Balancing

Ideally, you should cleanse and balance all your chakras every day using a chakra cleansing meditation. If you do not have the time, try starting three times a week. Every time you cleanse and balance your chakras, you ignite them and open them to receive energy from the Universe.

Try to work on your chakras in a comfortable place where you will not be disturbed. It is essential to focus on each of the seven chakras one at a time. Start with the root chakra and work your way up to your crown chakra. Allow each chakra to strengthen, become more stable, and for you to become familiar with it before you move on to the next.

When your chakras are aligned and working correctly, your energy flows, creating the physical, mental, spiritual, and emotional life you desire. The length of time you will start feeling this is different for everyone. The more you practice working on your chakras and make it a daily habit, the sooner you will see results.

When you are feeling off, ask yourself, "How am I feeling right now? Where in my body am I feeling troubled and not balanced"? For example, if you feel pain or heaviness in your heart, focus on working on your heart chakra until you feel a shift, feel balanced, and better. If you feel unsettled in your stomach and digestion, focus on your solar plexus until it feels settled.

Chapter 2
Understanding Ho'oponopono

Ho'oponopono is a simple practice with a long history. The word "ho'o" means "cause" in Hawaiian, while "ponopono" means "perfection." The term "Ho'oponopono" means "correct a mistake" or "make it right." Ho'oponopono is an ancient spiritual practice that originated in Hawaii and, before that, from the South Pacific's Polynesian Islands

It was used as a ceremonial practice to help islands settle their differences with one another. Later it was adapted to help with cooperation and forgiveness between individuals and communities. Like chakra work, it is a beneficial and straightforward method for healing and transformation". (What is Ho'oponopono? - Psychic Elements - Psychics Blog:

https://psychicelements.com/blog/what-is-hooponopono/)

How Does Ho'oponopono Work?

Ho'oponopono focuses on reconciliation and forgiveness by going within yourself to heal, not focusing on someone else to forgive. You only have control of yourself, not others. In our vibrational, connected Universe, any good you send out is received back to yourself. It may be difficult to accept, but you are ultimately responsible for your choices, life, and everything you experience.

Ho'oponopono is like pressing the reset button. It is a spiritual cleanser. You can use it daily just like you would take a shower and remove any unwanted debris off you. It washes away the negative energy accumulated, removing negative feelings towards yourself or others, bringing you to a neutral state. It is also a great tool to use for resetting and balancing your emotions.

Evidence shows a disruption to the emotional balance, causes illness. "In perhaps the most exciting development of all, a new field has emerged which is starting to combine the latest in neurosciences with the latest in immunology to provide the scientific basis for understanding relationships between emotions and disease once explored only in clinical settings." https://www.nlm.nih.gov/exhibition/emotions/frontiers.htmlPracticing Ho'oponopono will help you maintain a healthy mind, body, and spirit.

The Four Components of Ho'oponopono

Ho'oponopono consists of four parts or phrases:

- Admitting responsibility, "I'm sorry."
- Asking for forgiveness, "Please forgive me."
- Expressing gratitude, "Thank you."
- Giving love, "I love you."

When you say these phrases out loud or to yourself, it is a connection between you and your higher power (Source/God/Spirit). For example, perhaps you are feeling upset, and you just want things to get back to normal. The communication is between yourself and the Divine. Yet, the intention and energy will also help the person or persons involved in the situation.

These four powerful phrases are said to do the cleaning and correcting to help us heal.

Here are the four simple steps from start to finish cleaning a problem in your life:

- Identify the problem. Ask yourself, what is it in me that is causing this issue? What is making me feel this way? What is triggering me to react this way?
- Use the four phrases to formulate your request.
- Send your request to The Divine, God, The Universe. Internally repeat the words silently to yourself when the problem arises.
- Repeat the request until the issue is taken care of; the feeling-reaction goes away.
- Have no expectations. TRUST.

How to Practice Ho'oponopono

Learn and practice the four steps and the phrases; I am sorry. Please forgive me. Thank you. I love you. You can use them in any order. As you mentally or verbally repeat them, hold the vision of what you are clearing out. If you hope for a reconciliation with someone, you can imagine your words going through you to them. If you want to heal, direct your energy to the Divine (God, Universe, whoever you consider your higher power).

When you say or think the words, it is essential to be open and feel all your emotions that arise. Allow yourself to experience any negative emotions draining from your mind and body. Feel the memories, pain, and any resistance seeping away. Hold the vision of the problem and what you want to accomplish. Repeat the steps and phrases until you feel calm, neutral, and balanced.

When to Use Ho'oponopono

You can use Ho'oponopono anytime, day or place. Be consistent with establishing a new healthy habit and daily routine.

Here are some ideas of when you can use it:

- When your child, student, or pet misbehaves or is not listening
- When you are experiencing difficulties with a coworker, family, partner, and friend
- When you are worried and stressed about finances
- When you are tired, worn out, and lacking energy

- When you cannot sleep and are feeling restless
- After, or even during, any argument, conflict, or disagreement
- When you feel depressed, sad, or anxious
- When you are feeling angry
- When you are sad
- When you are scared
- When you are fearful
- When you can't focus

I hope you have a clearer understanding of how chakras and Ho'oponopono can work in your life. In the following chapters, you will learn how to utilize and implement these simple and powerful healing modalities to transform your life, beginning with the root chakra.

Root Chakra

Chapter 3
Root Chakra

I am safe and secure.
I am grounded.
I am abundant in all things.
I belong.

In your first week, you are learning about your root or base chakra. You start with your root chakra because it is at the very bottom of all your chakras and the function of the other chakras relies on the health of the root chakra. It is like the roots of a tree or the foundation of a building. It must be strong to support the rest of your chakras, allow energy to flow into them, and keep them healthy.

Location:

Your root chakra is between your perineum (the space between the anus and scrotum in the male and between the anus and the vulva in the female) and straight down between your feet.

Areas of the physical body:

- Spinal column
- Feet
- Legs
- Lower back
- Colon
- Varicose veins
- Hips

Characteristics:

- Survival
- Endurance
- Will to live
- Physical health
- Abundance
- GroundingStability
- Having basic needs met (food, shelter, sleep, etc.)
- Safety
- Security
- Manifesting
- Belonging to a community, family, and here on earth.

Focus and Meaning:

- Physical functioning

- Physical sensation
- Grounding

Out of alignment:

- Financial lack
- Lack of abundance
- Disconnection
- Fear of change
- Eating disorders
- Excessive negativity
- Spending too much money
- Physical issues with feet, legs, lower back, colon, varicose veins, and adrenal glands

Ways to Nourish Your Root Chakra

Crystals:

- Obsidian
- Jet
- Hematite
- Red Carnelian
- Red Jasper
- Bloodstone
- Black Tourmaline

Essential Oils:

- Patchouli
- Frankincense
- Cypress

Element:

The root chakra is associated with the earth. Any time you can spend in nature and surround yourself with people who love you and support you helps this chakra.

Movement:

- All forms of activities
- Any type of exercise
- Stretching
- Dancing
- Find an environment in which you feel good and at home
- Walk barefoot in the sand, dirt, or grass or sit or lie on it
- Gardening
- Hugging a tree

Color Therapy:

- Consider adding red to your wardrobe
- Cover-up in a red blanket

- Paint a canvas red or draw a picture with red in it and place it where you can see it every day
- Place some red flowers in your house

Nutrition:

- Eat root vegetables, potatoes, beets, carrots, onion, garlic, radish and parsnips, ginger, turmeric, and turnips.
- Eat red foods, strawberries, apples, watermelon, raspberries, tomatoes, pomegranates, red cabbage, and red peppers

Age it develops:

1-7 years old

Assignment:

Choose at least one way to nourish your chakra from the list above to start healing and supporting your root chakra this week. Ideally, you should practice daily, but if you cannot do that, start with a minimum of three times a week to start feeling a difference.

Self-Assessment:

Ask yourself these questions to see if you are in or out of alignment with your root chakra. Answer the questions the best you can in the space provided or use your journal, focusing on where you are right now in your healing. There are additional questions in Appendix A for further exploration.

Journaling is a great tool to track your chakra's health, your thoughts, feelings, and your progress when you decide to repeat these exercises in the future.

- Do I feel grounded, centered, and balanced in my physical body and my life? If not, what are some steps I can take to feel more balanced in my life?

- Do I spend time outside, take time to unplug from social media, and feel connected with nature? If not, what are some steps I can take to accomplish this?

- Do I look after my physical body through a proper diet, relaxation, adequate rest, and exercise? If not, what steps can I take to get more rest, sleep, and eat healthier?

- Do I feel that I belong to a community or tribe? If not, what are some steps I can take to start feeling like I belong?

- Do I live in an environment I love, where I feel safe, secure, and at home? If not, what are some steps I can take to feel loved and safe?

Ho'oponopono Activity

Review your answers to the above self-assessment. Choose the questions you want to focus on to improve your life using the Ho'oponopono phrase for each of them and write them out.

Remember, you are saying these words for YOU, not for another person that made you feel, think, or act a certain way. We are all one energy. You heal yourself; you remedy the situation.

Example:

"I am sorry. I forgive myself that I attract unnecessary drama into my life. Thank you for the lesson learned. I love you".

If you cannot forgive, thank, or love yourself right now, then start with, "I wish I could forgive myself. I wish I could thank myself. I wish I could love myself." It is just as powerful and effective.

Go ahead and write your responses in your journal or the space provided:

Root Chakra Meditation

You can do this meditation as many times in the day as you need to. Have a designated time to establish a consistent routine if you can.

Before you begin, sit, stand, or lay in a quiet place where you will not be disturbed for at least 15 minutes.

Close your eyes and take ten deep breaths, inhaling and exhaling slowly to help calm your mind.

Continue to breathe in and out and focus on your breathing.

Continue to breathe and now focus on the area of your root chakra.

Imagine a bubble slowly coming toward you that is full of the color red.

As it gets closer, take a deep breath, and allow yourself to breathe in the bubble and let the color flow into your root chakra area.

If you are having a hard time imagining this, simply put your hand on your pelvic area and breathe. Your intention and focus are the most important.

As you continue to breathe, let go of all your tension, anxiety, and fears as you exhale.

Continue letting the color fill up your chakra area, cleansing it, balancing it, and healing it.

In this state of calmness, focus on your chakra and say either out loud or in your mind the Ho'oponopono phrase; "I am sorry, please forgive me, I love you, and thank you," to help accelerate the healing process.

As you say, the Ho'oponopono phrase, make sure you are really "feeling" your emotions. You may repeat this as many times as you feel needed until you feel calm.

When you are ready, open your eyes.

Sacral Chakra

Chapter 4
Sacral Chakra

I allow my emotions to flow through me fully.
I love my sensuality.
I reawaken and ignite my passion.
I weave creativity into my life.

How did the first week go working on your root chakra? Did you feel any energy shifts within you? Did you notice any positive changes in your life or your health? If you feel like you need more time to work on your root chakra, go ahead and spend more time doing so before proceeding to your sacral chakra in the second week. There is no rush to get through all seven chakras in seven weeks.

In this second week, you are learning about your sacral chakra. The sacral chakra is your second chakra in your anatomy. It oversees your ability to manifest what you desire, your sensual, sexual, and creative expression. It is a powerful magnet when it is balanced, flowing, and energized.

Location:

It is in the sacrum area, just below the level of the navel.

Areas of the physical body:

- Lower abdomen
- Lower back
- Pelvis
- Reproductive system
- Kidneys
- Bladder
- The upper part of the large intestine (colon)

Characteristics:

- Emotions
- Feelings
- Relationships
- Expression of sexuality
- Expression of sensuality
- Creativity
- Empathy
- Desire
- Pleasure
- Boundaries

Focus and Meaning:

Feelings and emotions

Out of alignment:

- Lack of desire
- Lack of creativity
- Lack of joy
- Being irresponsible
- Overly emotional or not feeling anything
- Having an addictive behavior
- Overindulgence in fantasies
- Sexual obsessions
- Codependency
- Fertility and sexuality issues
- Gynecological problems
- Feelings of shame or guilt.

Ways To Nourish Your Sacral Chakra

Crystals:

- Garnet
- Ruby
- Tiger's Eye
- Orange and coral calcite
- Citrine
- Orange carnelian
- Orange aventurine

Element:

The sacral chakra is associated with water; swimming or spending time by water like lakes, rivers, pools, and oceans are beneficial. Also, being creative by exploring new things that please you: writing, painting, music.

Essential Oils:

- Ylang Ylang Oil
- Clary sage
- Sandalwood

Movement:

- Massages
- Hugs
- Dancing
- Exercise
- Sexual and sensual expression

Color Therapy:

- Consider adding orange to your wardrobe
- Cover-up in an orange blanket
- Paint a canvas orange or draw a picture with orange in it and place it where you can see it every day
- Place some orange flowers in your house

Nutrition:

- Eat orange foods, oranges, carrots, pumpkins, melons, mangos, and orange peppers.
- Seafood

Age it Develops:

8-14 years old

Assignment:

Choose at least one way to nourish your chakra from the list above to start healing and supporting your sacral chakra this week. Ideally, you should practice daily, but if you cannot do that, start with a minimum of three times a week to start feeling a difference.

Self-Assessment:

Ask yourself these questions to see if you are in or out of alignment with your root chakra. Answer the questions the best you can in the space provided or in your journal, focusing on where you are right now in your healing. There are additional questions in Appendix A for further exploration.

Journaling is a great tool to track your chakra's health, your thoughts, feelings, and your progress when you decide to repeat these exercises in the future.

- Am I willing to create more experiences in my life and find out more about myself? What are some steps I can take to achieve this?

- Do I enjoy my life? What are some steps I can take to achieve feeling more joy and pleasure?

- Do I feel good about myself and my gender? If not, what are some steps I can take to achieve this?

- Can I express myself sexually and sensually? If not, what steps can I take to learn how to feel into my sexuality and sensuality?

- Am I sexually fulfilled? If not, what are some steps I can take to achieve this?

Ho'oponopono Activity

Review your answers to the above self-assessment. Choose the questions you want to focus on to improve your life using the Ho'oponopono phrase for each of them and write them out.

Remember, you are saying these words for YOU, not for another person that made you feel, think, or act a certain way. We are all one energy. You heal yourself; you remedy the situation.

Example:

"I am sorry. Please forgive me for not expressing myself creatively and sharing my passion. Thank you for the opportunity to be able to express myself creatively. I love you".

If you cannot forgive, thank, or love yourself right now, then start with, "I wish I could forgive myself. I wish I could thank myself. I wish I could love myself." It is just as powerful and effective.

Go ahead and write your responses in your journal or the space provided:

Sacral Chakra Meditation

You can do this meditation as many times in the day as you need to. Have a designated time to establish a consistent routine if you can.

Before you begin, sit, stand, or lay in a quiet place where you will not be disturbed for at least 15 minutes.

Close your eyes and take ten deep breaths, inhaling and exhaling slowly to help calm your mind.

Continue to breathe in and out and focus on your breathing.

Continue to breathe and now focus on the area of your sacral chakra.

Imagine a bubble slowly coming toward you that is full of the color orange.

As it gets closer, take a deep breath, and allow yourself to breathe in the bubble, and let the color orange flow into your sacral chakra area.

If you have a hard time imagining this, simply put your hand on your upper abdomen area and breathe. Your intention and focus are the most important.

As you continue to breathe, let go of all your tension, anxiety, and fears as you exhale.

Continue letting the color fill up your chakra area, cleansing it, balancing it, and healing it.

In this state of calmness, focus on your chakra and say either out loud or in your mind the Ho'oponopono phrase, "I am

sorry, forgive me, I love you, and thank you," to help accelerate the healing process.

As you say the Ho'oponopono phrase, make sure you are really "feeling" into your emotions. You may repeat this as many times as you feel needed until you feel calm.

When you are ready, open your eyes.

Solar Plexus Chakra

Chapter 5
Solar Plexus Chakra

I am confident in all that I do.
I stand up for myself.
I always respect myself.
I am healthy and courageous.
I feel my power.

How did your second week go working on your sacral chakra? If you feel like you need more time to work on your sacral chakra, go ahead and spend more time doing so before proceeding to your solar plexus chakra for the third week.

In this third week, you are learning all about your solar plexus, your third chakra. It is your energy center that generates your self-esteem, confidence, and self-empowerment. It helps you to stand up for what you want, what is right for you, and for you to live it.

Location:

It is located above your navel and below your sternum.

Areas of the physical body:

- Pancreas
- Mid-back
- Upper abdomen
- Stomach
- Liver
- Gallbladder
- Spleen
- Digestive system

Characteristics:

- Personal will power
- Energy
- Metabolism
- Self-Esteem
- Self-discipline
- Social Identity
- Happiness
- Ambition
- Independence

Focus and Meaning:

Your moral code, ethics, standing up for yourself, and what you believe.

Out of alignment:

- Low self-esteem or self-confidence
- Feeling unhappy
- Fear rejection or criticism
- Overly controlling
- Passive
- Procrastination
- Digestion issues
- Anxiety
- Lacking clarity and direction
- Panic attacks
- Ulcers
- Liver problems
- Adrenal and chronic fatigue
- Irritable bowel syndrome
- Eating disorders

Ways To Nourish Your Solar Plexus Chakra

Element:

The solar plexus chakra is associated with fire and sunlight. Sitting around a bonfire or soaking up bright sunlight will help support this chakra.

Crystals:

- Amber
- Yellow Calcite
- Citrine
- Tiger's eye
- Yellow tourmaline

Essential Oils:

- Neroli
- Geranium
- Cinnamon
- Lemongrass
- Candlewood
- Rosemary

Color Therapy:

- Consider adding yellow to your wardrobe
- Cover-up in a yellow blanket
- Paint a canvas yellow or draw a picture with yellow in it and place it where you can see it every day
- Place some yellow flowers in your house

Nutrition:

- Eat yellow foods, bananas, pineapple, squash, yellow peppers, yellow zucchini, ginger, turmeric, and corn.

Age when it develops:

15-21 years old

Assignment:

Choose at least one way to nourish your chakra from the list above to start healing and supporting your solar plexus chakra this week. Ideally, you should practice daily, but if you cannot do that, start with a minimum of three times a week to start feeling a difference.

Self-Assessment:

Ask yourself these questions to see if you are in or out of alignment with your solar plexus chakra. Answer the questions the best you can in the space provided or in your journal, focusing on where you are right now in your healing. There are additional questions in Appendix A for further exploration.

Journaling is a great tool to track your chakra's health, your thoughts, feelings, and your progress when you decide to repeat these exercises in the future.

- Can I stand up for what I believe? If not, what steps can I take to start standing up for myself?

- Do I have healthy self-esteem and feel confident? If not, what steps can I take to strengthen my self-esteem and confidence?

- Am I able to stay balanced and sure of myself despite other people's thoughts and emotions? If not, what steps can I take not to let others impact how I feel?

- Can I focus on a task and follow it through? If not, what steps can I take to start staying more focused?

- Do I have a sense of what is right or wrong for me? If not, what steps can I take to start being more aware of the choices I make?

Ho'oponopono Activity

Review your answers to the above self-assessment. Choose the questions you want to focus on to improve your life using the Ho'oponopono phrase for each of them and write them out.

Remember, you are saying these words for YOU, not for another person that made you feel, think, or act a certain way.

Example:

"I am sorry. I forgive myself that I experience panic attacks and anxiety. Thank you. I love you".

If you cannot forgive, thank or love yourself right now, then start with, "I wish I could forgive myself. I wish I could thank myself. I wish I could love myself." It is just as powerful and effective.

Go ahead and write your responses in your journal or the space provided:

Solar Plexus Chakra Meditation

You can do this meditation as many times in the day as you need to. Have a designated time to establish a consistent routine if you can.

Before you begin, sit, stand, or lay in a quiet place where you will not be disturbed for at least 15 minutes.

Close your eyes and take ten deep breaths, inhaling and exhaling slowly to help calm your mind.

Continue to breathe in and out and focus on your breathing.

Continue to breathe and now focus on the area of your solar plexus chakra.

Imagine a bubble slowly coming toward you that is full of the color yellow.

As it gets closer, take a deep breath, and allow yourself to breathe in the bubble, and let the color yellow flow into your solar plexus chakra area.

If you have a hard time imagining this, simply put your hand on your upper stomach, above your belly button, and breathe. Your intention and focus are the most important.

As you continue to breathe, let go of all your tension, anxiety, and fears as you exhale.

Continue letting the color fill up your chakra area, cleansing it, balancing it, and healing it.

In this state of calmness, focus on your chakra and say either out loud or in your mind the Ho'oponopono phrase, "I am

sorry, forgive me, I love you, and thank you," to help accelerate the healing process.

As you say the Ho'oponopono phrase, make sure you are really "feeling" into your emotions. You may repeat this as many times as you feel needed until you feel calm.

When you are ready, open your eyes.

Heart Chakra

Chapter 6
Heart Chakra

I love myself.
I am kind to myself.
I can let go of the past.
I forgive myself and others.

You are now moving up into the higher chakras. Hopefully, your lower chakras, root, sacral, and solar plexus feel in alignment and working correctly. How do you feel after working on your solar plexus chakra? If you feel like you need more time to work on your solar plexus chakra, go ahead and spend more time doing so before you proceed to your heart chakra for the fourth week.

Your heart chakra is the fourth chakra in your body. It is one of the most, if not the most important, chakra. Your solar plexus and your heart chakra work closely together. With your solar plexus, you learned about yourself and your self-esteem, and your place of strength. Your heart chakra deepens your ability to be more compassionate, connect with others, balance, trust, and become a vessel for love.

Location:

The center of your chest

Areas of the physical body:

- Heart
- Lung
- Thymus
- Chest
- Shoulders
- Upper back
- Arms
- Hands and fingers
- Blood
- Vagus nerve
- Circulatory system

Characteristics:

- Giving and receiving love
- Self-love
- Understanding
- Trust
- Hope
- Compassion

- Forgiveness
- Acceptance of self and others
- Taking responsibility for yourself

Focus and Meaning:

- Love
- Transformation
- A bridge between higher and lower chakras

Out of alignment:

- Fear of intimacy
- Unable to forgive
- Lack of self-love
- Lack of empathy
- Feeling jealous
- Difficulty trusting others
- Selfishness
- Asthma and other breathing issues
- Allergies
- Heart issues
- Compromised immune system
- Breast cancer

Ways To Nourish Your Throat Chakra

Elements:

The heart chakra is associated with air, so breathing deeply and slowly, will help clear the energy at this level.

Crystals:

- Malachite
- Rose Quartz
- Pink Quartz
- Clear Quartz
- Jade
- Green Calcite

Essential Oils:

- Chamomile
- Cypress
- Lavender
- Wild orange
- Rose
- Neroli
- Jasmine

Color therapy:

- Consider adding green to your wardrobe
- Cover-up in a green blanket
- Paint a canvas green or draw a picture with green in it and place it where you can see it every day
- Place some green plants in your house

Nutrition:

- Eat green foods, grapes, cucumbers, broccoli, avocado, zucchini, apples, Brussels sprouts, peas, and leafy greens like kale or spinach

When it develops:

21-28 years old

Assignment:

Choose at least one way to nourish your chakra from the list above to start healing and supporting your heart chakra this week. Ideally, you should practice daily, but if you cannot do that, start with a minimum of three times a week to start feeling a difference.

Self-Assessment:

Ask yourself these questions to see if you are in or out of alignment with your heart chakra. Answer the questions the best you can in the space provided or in your journal, focusing on where you are right now in your healing. There are additional questions in Appendix A for further exploration.

Journaling is a great tool to track your chakra's health, your thoughts, feelings, and your progress when you decide to repeat these exercises in the future.

- Do I practice loving myself? If not, what steps can I take to start loving myself?

- Do I feel a deep connection with others? If not, what steps can I take to start reaching out to others and feeling more connected?

- Can I forgive and accept myself and others? If not, what steps can I take to work toward this?

- Have I let go of feelings of betrayal, disappointment, or anger? If not, what steps can I take to resolve the past and move on to heal?

- Do I have a healthy immune system? If not, what steps can I take to start?

Ho'oponopono Activity

Review your answers to the above self-assessment. Choose the questions you want to focus on to improve your life using the Ho'oponopono phrase for each of them and write them out.

Remember, you are saying these words for YOU, not for another person that made you feel, think, or act a certain way.

Example:

"I am sorry. I forgive myself that I am unable to love myself. Thank you. I love you".

If you cannot forgive, thank, or love yourself right now, then start with, "I wish I could forgive myself. I wish I could thank myself. I wish I could love myself." It is just as powerful and effective.

Go ahead and write your responses in your journal or the space provided:

Heart Chakra Meditation

You can do this meditation as many times in the day as you need to. Have a designated time to establish a consistent routine if you can.

Before you begin, sit, stand, or lay in a quiet place where you will not be disturbed for at least 15 minutes.

Close your eyes and take ten deep breaths, inhaling and exhaling slowly to help calm your mind.

Continue to breathe in and out and focus on your breathing.

Continue to breathe and now focus on the area of your heart chakra.

Imagine a bubble slowly coming toward you that is full of the color green.

As it gets closer, take a deep breath, and allow yourself to breathe in the bubble, and let the color green flow into your heart chakra area.

If you have a hard time imagining this, simply put your hand on your heart area and breathe. Your intention and focus are the most important.

As you continue to breathe, let go of all of your tension, anxiety, and fears as you exhale.

Continue letting the color fill up your chakra area, cleansing it, balancing it, and healing it.

In this state of calmness, focus on your chakra and say either out loud or in your mind the Ho'oponopono phrase, "I am

sorry, forgive me, I love you, and thank you," to help accelerate the healing process.

As you say the Ho'oponopono phrase, make sure you are really "feeling" into your emotions. You may repeat this as many times as you feel needed until you feel calm.

When you are ready, open your eyes.

Throat Chakra

Chapter 7
Throat Chakra

I speak up for myself.
I express my authentic self with clarity and confidence.
I listen to others.
I share and communicate respectfully with myself and others.

How did your fourth week go working on your heart chakra? If you feel like you need more time to work on your heart chakra, go ahead and spend more time doing so before proceeding to your throat chakra for the fifth week.

Your throat chakra is the fifth chakra in your anatomy. This chakra helps with your ability to express your needs and desires, open and honest communication, creativity, and surrendering personal will to divine will. This chakra has a natural connection with your sacral chakra.

Location:

Throat area

Areas of the physical body:

- Parathyroid
- Thyroid
- Bronchial
- Pharyngeal and brachial plexus
- Mouth
- Jaws
- Tongue
- Pharynx
- Palate
- Lungs
- Ears
- Neck

Characteristics:

- Governs your drive to express yourself authentically and originally to speak out
- Oversees your self-determination and ability to speak your truth
- Communication; listening and talking; verbal and non-verbal
- Realizing your purpose
- Good sense of timing
- Creativity

Focus and Meaning:

Alignment with Divine Will and purification

Out of alignment:

- Inability to speak one's truth
- Fear of speaking
- Difficulty expressing feelings
- Talking too much
- Gossiping
- Insecurity
- Unable to keep secrets
- Thyroid problems
- Sore throat
- Mouth ulcers
- Neck ache
- Hearing issues
- Earache

Ways To Nourish Your Throat Chakra

Element:

The throat chakra is associated with your etheric body (like spirit). Sitting in an open space under a clear sky during the day or night is a fabulous way to get this energy flowing appropriately.

Crystals:

- Aquamarine
- Lapis Lazuli
- Turquoise
- Amazonite

Movement:

- Singing
- Chanting
- Meaningful Discussions
- Writing
- Listening
- Creative expression
- Acting
- Performing
- Public speaking

Essential Oils:

- Peppermint
- Bergamot
- Basil

Color Therapy:

- Consider adding blue to your wardrobe

- Cover-up in a blue blanket
- Paint a canvas blue or draw a picture with blue in it and place it where you can see it every day
- Place some blue flowers in your house

Nutrition:

- Eat blue foods, blueberries, currants, dragon fruit, and kelp.
- Other foods good for your throat: herbal tea, lemon, raw honey

Age it develops:

29-35 years old

Assignment:

Choose at least one way to nourish your chakra from the list above to start healing and supporting your throat chakra this week. Ideally, you should practice daily, but if you cannot do that, start with a minimum of three times a week to start feeling a difference.

Self-Assessment:

Ask yourself these questions to see if you are in or out of alignment with your throat chakra. Answer the questions the best you can in the space provided or in your journal, focusing on where you are right now in your healing. There are additional questions in Appendix A for further exploration.

Journaling is a great tool to track your chakra's health, your thoughts, feelings, and your progress when you decide to repeat these exercises in the future.

- Can I openly and honestly communicate how I feel? If not, why? What steps can I take to start?

- Do I speak up if I feel misunderstood? If not, what steps can I take to clarify what I have said?

- Do I speak too much or talk inappropriately? If so, how can I control what I am saying?

- Am I able to express my creative ideas and inspirations? If not, how can I start being more creative in my daily life?

- Do I listen to other people and allow others to have their point of view? If not, what steps can I take to assure others feel important and heard when they talk to me?

Ho'oponopono Activity

Review your answers to the above self-assessment. Choose the questions you want to focus on to improve your life using the Ho'oponopono phrase for each of them and write them out.

Remember, you are saying these words for YOU, not for another person that made you feel, think, or act a certain way.

Example:

"I am sorry. I forgive myself that I am unable to communicate openly and honestly. Thank you. I love you".

If you cannot forgive, thank, or love yourself right now, then start with, "I wish I could forgive myself. I wish I could thank myself. I wish I could love myself." It is just as powerful and effective.

Go ahead and write your responses in your journal or the space provided:

Throat Chakra Meditation

You can do this meditation as many times in the day as you need to. Have a designated time to establish a consistent routine if you can.

Before you begin, sit, stand, or lay in a quiet place where you will not be disturbed for at least 15 minutes.

Close your eyes and take ten deep breaths, inhaling, and exhaling slowly to help calm your mind.

Continue to breathe in and out and focus on your breathing.

Continue to breathe and now focus on the area of your throat chakra.

Imagine a bubble slowly coming toward you that is full of the color blue.

As it gets closer, take a deep breath, and allow yourself to breathe in the bubble, and let the color blue flow into your throat chakra area.

If you have a hard time imagining this, simply put your hand on your throat area and breathe. Your intention and focus are the most important.

As you continue to breathe, let go of all your tension, anxiety, and fears as you exhale.

Continue letting the color fill up your chakra area, cleansing it, balancing it, and healing it.

In this state of calmness, focus on your chakra and say either out loud or in your mind the Ho'oponopono phrase, "I am

sorry, forgive me, I love you, and thank you," to help accelerate the healing process.

As you say the Ho'oponopono phrase, make sure you are really "feeling" into your emotions. You may repeat this as many times as you feel needed until you feel calm.

When you are ready, open your eyes.

Third Eye Chakra

Chapter 8
Third Eye Chakra

I am one with the Universe.
I always honor and follow my intuition.
I invite sacred transformation.
It is safe for me to see the truth.

How did your fifth week go working on your throat chakra? If you feel like you need more time to work on your throat chakra, go ahead and spend more time doing so before proceeding to your third eye chakra for the sixth week.

Your third eye is your sixth chakra in your body. With this chakra, you will begin exploring your higher consciousness even further, expanding your awareness of what lies beyond the earth's plane.

In this chakra, you will seek to develop your insight, spirituality, awareness, and intuition. By continuing to practice, you will be able to learn how to "open your third eye."

Location:

Between your eyebrows, in the middle of your head.

Areas of the physical body:

- Oversees the physical space of the head
- Brain
- Pineal gland
- Pituitary gland
- Ears
- Eyes

Characteristics:

- It is an instrument to look and feel beyond the physical senses into the realm of other energies to help you transcend this earth plane
- Awaken your intuitive sensibility and inner perception
- Associated with the other dimensions, as well as the realm of spirits
- Ability to self-reflect
- Seeks higher love
- Nurture and protect all life
- Compassion
- Intuition
- Vision and imagination

Focus and Meaning:

Connection to wisdom and insight and your ability to perceive

Out of alignment:

- Overly sensitive to sounds
- Drained from other's energy
- Not trusting your intuition
- Not being able to establish a vision for yourself
- Rejection of everything spiritual or beyond the usual
- Lack of clarity
- Migraines and headaches
- Vision problems
- Sinus and nasal issues
- Learning difficulties
- Sleep issues

Ways To Nourish Your Crown Chakra

Element:

The crown chakra connects all the elements. Focus on connecting your whole self by spending time in thought:

- Meditating
- Chanting
- Prayer

- Watching the sky, clouds, and stars
- Being present and still

Crystals:

- Clear quartz
- Amethyst Selenite

Essential Oils:

- Frankincense
- Myrrh
- Cedarwood

Color Therapy:

- Consider adding indigo (blue-violet) to your wardrobe
- Cover-up in an indigo blanket
- Paint a canvas indigo or draw a picture with indigo in it and place it where you can see it every day
- Place some blue-violet flowers in your house

Nutrition:

- Eat foods with indigo (blue-violet) color, purple kale, grapes, purple potatoes, eggplant, and blackberries.
- Omega 3 foods: any type of fish, walnuts, chia seeds

Age when it develops:

36-42 years old

Assignment:

Choose at least one way to nourish your chakra from the list above to start healing and supporting your third eye chakra this week. Ideally, you should practice daily, but if you cannot do that, start with a minimum of three times a week to start feeling a difference.

Self-Assessment:

Ask yourself these questions to see if you are in or out of alignment with your third eye chakra. Answer the questions the best you can in the space provided or in your journal, focusing on where you are right now in your healing. There are additional questions in Appendix A for further exploration.

Journaling is a great tool to track your chakra's health, your thoughts, feelings, and your progress when you decide to repeat these exercises in the future.

- Do I listen to my intuition and follow intuitive hunches? If not, what steps can I take to start practicing my intuition?

- Do I have a difficult time focusing and concentrating? If so, what steps can I take to help with this?

- Do I allow myself to use my imagination and be creative? If not, what steps can I take to start being more imaginative and creative?

- Do I have a poor memory? If so, what can I do to help my memory?

Ho'oponopono Activity

Review your answers to the above self-assessment. Choose the questions you want to focus on to improve your life using the Ho'oponopono phrase for each of them and write them out.

Remember, you are saying these words for YOU, not for another person that made you feel, think, or act a certain way.

Example:

"I am sorry. I forgive myself for not allowing myself to use my imagination and trust my intuition. Thank you. I love you".

If you cannot forgive, thank, or love yourself right now, then start with, "I wish I could forgive myself. I wish I could thank myself. I wish I could love myself." It is just as powerful and effective.

Go ahead and write your responses in your journal or the space provided:

Wendi M. Lindenmuth

Third Eye Chakra Meditation

You can do this meditation as many times in the day as you need to. Having a designated time helps to establish a routine and be consistent.

Before you begin, sit, stand, or lay in a quiet place where you will not be disturbed for at least 15 minutes.

Close your eyes and take ten deep breaths, inhaling and exhaling slowly to help calm your mind.

Continue to breathe in and out and focus on your breathing.

Continue to breathe and focus on the area of your third eye chakra.

Imagine a bubble slowly coming toward you that is full of the color indigo.

As it gets closer, take a deep breath, and allow yourself to breathe in the bubble, and let the color indigo flow into your third eye chakra area.

If you have a hard time imagining this, simply put your hand on your forehead area and breathe. Your intention and focus are the most important.

As you continue to breathe, let go of all your tension, anxiety, and fears as you exhale.

Continue letting the color fill up your chakra area, cleansing it, balancing it, and healing it.

In this state of calmness, focus on your chakra and say either out loud or in your mind the Ho'oponopono phrase, "I am

sorry, forgive me, I love you, and thank you," to help accelerate the healing process.

As you say the Ho'oponopono phrase, make sure you are really "feeling" into your emotions. You may repeat this as many times as you feel needed until you feel calm.

When you are ready, open your eyes.

Crown Chakra

Chapter 9
Crown Chakra

I go beyond my limiting beliefs and accept myself.
I am infinite and at one with the Universe.
I am enlightened.

How did your sixth week go working on your third eye chakra? If you feel like you need more time to work on your third eye chakra, go ahead and spend more time doing so before proceeding to your crown chakra for the last week.

The crown chakra is your seventh chakra. This chakra helps you experience enlightenment and connection with the Divine and trust and believe you are one with all that is. When you accept and trust you are part of everything and everyone, you begin to live your life by being genuinely aligned with your purpose and path.

Location:
The top of your head or slightly above.

Areas of the physical body:

- Upper brain
- Pineal gland
- Pituitary gland
- Nervous system
- Hypothalamus

Characteristics:

- Oneness with the Universe and Divinity
- Surrendering to divinity
- Enlightenment
- Knowing your soul's purpose
- Awareness of higher Consciousness
- Awareness of what is sacred

Focus and Meaning:

To move beyond materialistic needs and trust and connect with the Universe. It is about experiencing the transcendence of your limitations, whether personal or bound to space and time, and opening the door to the Divine.

Out of alignment:

- Lack of joy
- Lack of purpose
- Feeling alone

- Feeling disconnected from your body
- Sleep issues
- Difficulty meditating
- Disconnected to spirit
- Obsessive attachment to spiritual matters
- Headaches and migraines
- Vertigo
- Hypersensitive
- Chronic tiredness
- Hopelessness
- Depression
- Lack of faith
- Closed-mindedness

Ways To Nourish Your Crown Chakra

Element:

The crown chakra connects all the elements. Focus on connecting your whole self by spending time in thought:

- Meditating
- Chanting
- Prayer
- Watching the sky, clouds, and stars
- Being present and still

Crystals:

- Clear quartz
- Amethyst Selenite

Essential Oils:

- Frankincense
- Myrrh
- Cedarwood

Color Therapy:

- Consider adding purple to your wardrobe
- Cover-up in a purple blanket
- Paint a canvas purple or draw a picture with purple in it and place it where you can see it every day
- Place some purple flowers in your house

Nutrition:

- Spiritual and mindfulness practices for your body, mind, and spirit will help nourish this chakra.
- The colors associated with the crown chakra are white and purple/violet. White foods: mushrooms, coconut, garlic, onion. Violet fruits and vegetables: passionfruit, eggplant, and red grapes.

Age it develops:

43-49 years old

Assignment:

Choose at least one way to nourish your chakra from the list above to start healing and supporting your crown chakra this week. Ideally, you should practice daily, but if you cannot do that, start with a minimum of three times a week to start feeling a difference.

Self-Assessment:

Ask yourself these questions to see if you are in or out of alignment with your crown chakra. Answer the questions the best you can in the space provided or in your journal, focusing on where you are right now in your healing. There are additional questions in Appendix A for further exploration.

Journaling is a great tool to track your chakra's health, your thoughts, feelings, and your progress when you decide to repeat these exercises in the future.

- Do I feel enlightened or have glimpsed how that feels? If not, what changes can I make to achieve this?

- Do I understand and feel connected to everything and everyone? If not, what steps can I take to begin understanding this?

- Can I sit quietly without the need to think or do something? If not, what steps can I take to change my routine and behavior to achieve this?

- Do I know how to be present, live in the moment, and not worry about the past or future? If not, what steps can I take to change this?

- Do I feel I have a purpose in life? If not, what steps can I take to start feeling essential and recognizing what makes me happy and brings joy into my life?

Ho'oponopono Activity

Review your answers to the above self-assessment. Choose the questions you want to focus on to improve your life using the Ho'oponopono phrase for each of them and write them out.

Remember, you are saying these words for YOU, not for another person that made you feel, think, or act a certain way.

Example:

"I am sorry. I forgive myself for not feeling connected to God, the Creator, and the Universe. Thank you. I love you".

If you cannot forgive, thank, or love yourself right now, then start with, "I wish I could forgive myself. I wish I could thank myself. I wish I could love myself." It is just as powerful and effective.

Go ahead and write your responses in your journal or the space provided:

Crown Chakra Meditation

You can do this meditation as many times in the day as you need to. Have a designated time to establish a consistent routine if you can.

Before you begin, sit, stand, or lay in a quiet place where you will not be disturbed for at least 15 minutes.

Close your eyes and take ten deep breaths, inhaling and exhaling slowly to help calm your mind.

Continue to breathe in and out and focus on your breathing.

Continue to breathe and focus on the area of your crown chakra.

Imagine a bubble slowly coming toward you that filled with the color purple.

As it gets closer, take a deep breath, and allow yourself to breathe in the bubble, and let the purple color flow into your crown chakra area.

If you are having a hard time imagining this, simply put your hand on your pelvic area and breathe. Your intention and focus are the most important.

As you continue to breathe, let go of all your tension, anxiety, and fears as you exhale.

Continue letting the color fill up your chakra area, cleansing it, balancing it, and healing it.

In this state of calmness, focus on your chakra and say either out loud or in your mind the Ho'oponopono phrase, "I am

sorry, forgive me, I love you, and thank you," to help accelerate the healing process.

As you say the Ho'oponopono phrase, make sure you are really "feeling" into your emotions. You may repeat this as many times as you feel needed until you feel calm.

When you are ready, open your eyes.

HEALING FROM WITHIN

Chapter 10
Using All of Your Chakras

Now that you have practiced and implemented balancing, cleansing, and healing your chakras for the past seven weeks, you are ready to work on all of them daily. Ideally, you should balance your chakras every day to maintain optimal health. Still, even a few times a week will be beneficial. You can work on your chakras before you get out of bed, during a lunch break, in the bathroom, or before bed. Find a time of day and location that works best for you.

I recommend checking in with your body daily and scan to see where you feel off, unbalanced, and unwell. If your throat feels sore, for example, then work on your throat chakra by nourishing it with the information you now have in the throat chakra chapter. If you are feeling less confident and need encouragement, work on your solar plexus. If you need some creative inspiration, work on your sacral chakra, and so on.

Below is a chakra meditation that incorporates all of your chakras. You can also find links to guided chakra meditations in the resource section of this book. If you are having difficulty doing this on your own, a guided meditation is beneficial to stay focused.

Chakra Healing Meditation

Before you begin, sit, stand, or lay in a quiet place where you will not be disturbed for at least 15 to 30 minutes.

Close your eyes and take ten deep breaths, inhaling and exhaling slowly to help calm your mind.

Continue to breathe in and out and focus on your breathing.

One at a time, imagine a bubble slowly coming toward you that is filled with each of the chakra colors, starting with red, orange, yellow, green, blue, indigo, and purple.

As each color gets closer, take a deep breath, and allow yourself to breathe in that specific color, and let it flow to the area where that chakra is located.

If you have a hard time imagining this, simply put your hand on the chakra area you are focused on and breathe. Your intention and focus are the most important.

As you continue to breathe, let go of all your tension, anxiety, and fears as you exhale.

Continue letting each color fill up your chakra area, cleansing it, balancing it, and healing it.

In this state of calmness, focus on each chakra and say either out loud or in your mind the Ho'oponopono phrase, "I am sorry, forgive me, I love you, and thank you," to help accelerate the healing process.

As you say the Ho'oponopono phrase, make sure you are really "feeling" into your emotions. You may repeat this as many times as you feel needed until you feel calm.

When you are ready, open your eyes.

Conclusion

Congratulations! You have completed seven weeks of healing your chakras with Ho'oponopono and journaling.

How are you feeling after seven weeks of working on yourself?

What have you learned about yourself?

What changes have you noticed in your personal and professional life?

How have you grown as an individual?

Will you implement new changes in your life? If so, like what?

How will you continue working on your inner self?

How will you ensure that your chakras are aligned, balanced, flowing correctly, and healthy physically, mentally, emotionally, and spiritually?

Although this book has come to an end, your healing journey from within has only just begun. As you continue working with your chakras and Ho'oponopono, do not be surprised if you start seeing your life and the world around you in a new positive light.

I encourage you to re-read this book and extend working on each chakra for a full month before moving on to the next chakra to strengthen and support each chakra even further.

I sincerely wish you all the best in your healing journey and send you a huge hug full of love, light, and Ho'oponopono.

Thank you with all my heart for showing up and being committed to improving your life and health.

You are important and deserve to have the tools to experience a wonderful and healthy life.

Love,

Wendi

Resources

- Chakra Meditation for all your chakras

https://www.youtube.com/watch?v=y8LIbeKQ60U

- Chakra Balancing and Healing Music

https://www.youtube.com/watch?v=Lju6h-C37hE

- Root Chakra

https://www.youtube.com/watch?v=35dT-fdDNd8&t=67s

- Sacral Chakra

https://www.youtube.com/watch?v=QcId1qEKGJo

- Solar Plexus Chakra

https://www.youtube.com/watch?v=6Sh1omf2v6o

- Heart Chakra

https://www.youtube.com/watch?v=5Yfeo3kPVSs&t=595s

- Throat Chakra

https://www.youtube.com/watch?v=ynnRsQIat0U

- Third Eye Chakra

https://www.youtube.com/watch?v=kBhHUxLcSPM

- Crown Chakra

https://www.youtube.com/watch?v=lLxSpW35ELY

- Ho'oponopono Meditations

https://www.youtube.com/watch?v=yDJYZXlsASg&t=859s

https://www.youtube.com/watch?v=VmX7RYOe_2s

- Emotions and Disease

https://www.nlm.nih.gov/exhibition/emotions/frontiers.html

What is Ho'oponopono? - Psychic Elements - Psychics Blog

https://psychicelements.com/blog/what-is-hooponopono/)

Appendix A

Additional Self-Assessment Questions for Each Chakra

Below are additional self-assessment questions to explore deeper into each chakra. I invite you to also do the Ho'oponopono activity with each one for extra healing and support.

Root Chakra

- Can I manifest and create what I need to live in this world? If I cannot, what are some steps I can take to change that?

- Do I have issues with my lower spine, legs, feet, hips, and large intestine? What are some steps I can take to get help for these issues?

- Do I have issues with chronic fatigue? If so, what are some steps I can take to start getting more rest and sleep?

- Am I overweight, obese, or underweight? If so, what are some steps I can take to help with my weight?

- Do I attract drama? If so, what are some steps I can take to help get away from the drama?

- Do I feel financially secure and abundant? If not, what are some steps I can take to achieve more abundance?

- Does life on earth feel like a burden? If so, what are some steps I can take to help it not feel like this way?

Ho'oponopono Activity

Review your answers to the above self-assessment. Choose the questions you want to focus on to improve your life using the Ho'oponopono phrase for each of them and write them out.

Remember, you are saying these words for YOU, not for another person that made you feel, think, or act a certain way.

Go ahead and write your responses in your journal or the space provided:

Sacral Chakra

- Do I have a negative attitude about sex? What steps can I take to start having a more positive attitude about sex?

- Am I obsessed with sexual thoughts or feelings? What steps can I take to keep my mind busy on other things besides sexual thoughts and feelings?

- Can I express myself creatively, or do I have a creative block? If not, what are some steps I can express myself more creatively?

- Do I make time for play and pleasure? If not, what are some steps you can take to explore this more?

- Am I passionate or excited about life? If not, what are some steps I can take to start feeling more excited?

- Do I have emotional boundary issues with others? If so, what steps can I take to set more defined boundaries?

- Do I have issues with my reproductive system, kidneys, bladder, and colon? If so, what steps can I take to get started healing them?

Ho'oponopono Activity

Review your answers to the above self-assessment. Choose the questions you want to focus on to improve your life using the Ho'oponopono phrase for each of them and write them out.

Remember, you are saying these words for YOU, not for another person that made you feel, think, or act a certain way.

Go ahead and write your responses in your journal or the space provided:

Wendi M. Lindenmuth

Solar Plexus Chakra

- Am I able to set appropriate boundaries? If not, what steps can I take to start making more defined boundaries to protect myself?

- Can I protect myself from feeling overly responsible for other people's lives, choices, and emotions? If not, what steps can I take to let go of the idea that I am only responsible for myself?

- Am I able to motivate myself and feel empowered? If not, what steps can I take to start doing the things I want and need to do?

- Do I suffer from digestive problems? If so, what steps can I take to improve my digestive system?

- Do I suffer from anxiety and panic attacks? If so, what steps can I take to start feeling better?

- Do I experience low energy and feel tired all the time? If so, what steps can I take to start improving my sleep and getting more rest?

- Do I feel ashamed of who I am? If so, what steps can I take to start loving and accepting myself?

Ho'oponopono Activity

Review your answers to the above self-assessment. Choose the questions you want to focus on to improve your life using the Ho'oponopono phrase for each of them and write them out.

Remember, you are saying these words for YOU, not for another person that made you feel, think, or act a certain way.

Go ahead and write your responses in your journal or the space provided:

Heart Chakra

- Can I accept other people for who they are, or do I always find fault in others? If not, what steps can I take to accept others as they are?

- Can I give and receive physical affection? If not, what is stopping me? What can I do to start showing respect to others?

- What does love and being loved unconditionally feel like for me?

- Can I love and be loved unconditionally, without strings attached? If not, why? What steps can I take to try?

- Do I have a fear of intimacy? If so, do I know why? What steps can I take to start feeling more comfortable with intimacy?

- Am I able to fully experience my emotions, or do I feel indifferent? If I have difficulty, what steps can I take to acknowledge my feelings?

- Do I have difficulty breathing? If so, what can I do to help breathe better?

- Do I have a healthy heart, chest, lungs, and circulatory system? If not, what steps can I take to address this and take care of myself?

Ho'oponopono Activity

Review your answers to the above self-assessment. Choose the questions you want to focus on to improve your life using the Ho'oponopono phrase for each of them and write them out.

Remember, you are saying these words for YOU, not for another person that made you feel, think, or act a certain way.

Go ahead and write your responses in your journal or the space provided:

Throat Chakra

- Do I have an outlet to express my authentic and individual self? If not, what are some things that I enjoy doing?

- Do I creatively express myself? If not, what are some ways I can show my true self through creativity?

- Do I have a fear of speaking? If so, what are some small steps I can take to start being more comfortable using my voice?

- Do I speak harshly to others? If so, how can I stop?

- Do I talk too much? What steps can I take to be aware of when I do and see why I do?

- Do I frequently have a sore throat? If so, what can I do to improve my immune system and get to the root cause of why?

- Do I have issues with my neck, throat, jaw, teeth, and thyroid problems? If so, what steps can I take to see why and to help support my body?

Ho'oponopono Activity

Review your answers to the above self-assessment. Choose the questions you want to focus on to improve your life using the Ho'oponopono phrase for each of them and write them out.

Remember, you are saying these words for YOU, not for another person that made you feel, think, or act a certain way.

Go ahead and write your responses in your journal or the space provided:

Wendi M. Lindenmuth

Third Eye Chakra

- Do I have problems with my physical health, sinuses, eyes, headaches, migraines, ears, neurological disturbances? If so, what steps can I take to get this checked out and start feeling healthy again?

- Do I have nightmares? If so, do I know why? What steps can I take to deal with this and to start sleeping better?

- Do I have extreme mood swings? If so, have I had my hormones checked? Have I been observant of what foods I have been eating that may cause them (sugar, colored dyes)?

- Do I feel paranoid? If so, is something causing me to feel this way? What helps me to feel better?

- Am I closed-minded? If so, why? What steps can I take to see things differently?

- Do I lack vision? If so, what is stopping me from creating my future and seeing how things can be different?

- Do I tend to live in a fantasy world? If so, why? How can I take steps to join the real world and not be afraid or uncomfortable?

Ho'oponopono Activity

Review your answers to the above self-assessment. Choose the questions you want to focus on to improve your life using the Ho'oponopono phrase for each of them and write them out.

Remember, you are saying these words for YOU, not for another person that made you feel, think, or act a certain way.

Go ahead and write your responses in your journal or the space provided:

Crown Chakra

- Am I afraid of dying? If so, what are my reasons why?

- Do I have an unhealthy attachment to my belongings or relationships? If so, why do I think I am, and how can I start letting go?

- Do I have an addictive relationship with spirituality? If so, how can I learn to be balanced in this world and with spirit?

- Do I search for answers outside myself? If so, how can I start learning to trust myself and find the answers within me?

- Do I suffer from dizziness, confusion, or neurological disorders? If so, what steps can I take to get this checked out to feel better?

- Do I suffer from hair loss and hormonal imbalances? If so, what steps can I take to get this checked out and address these issues?

Ho'oponopono Activity

Review your answers to the above self-assessment. Choose the questions you want to focus on to improve your life using the Ho'oponopono phrase for each of them and write them out.

Remember, you are saying these words for YOU, not for another person that made you feel, think, or act a certain way.

Go ahead and write your responses in your journal or the space provided:

Acknowledgments

First and foremost, a heartfelt thank you to God for always supporting and believing in me. You dared me to reach beyond what I thought I was capable of and create this book with your love, trust, and guidance.

A special thank you to Michelle Guajardo for her continued inspiration, support, and encouragement to get this book written and published. Also, for helping me with my designs. I appreciate you every day.

Once again, Piers Knightingale helped me with my editing. I am grateful for your support and for sharing our ideas and passion for reading and writing with each other.

A special thank you to my support team, my dogs, Auggie, Nike, Wren, and Rusty, for all the love, laughter, snuggles, naps, and kisses while I wrote this book.

Much gratitude for my husband. He patiently listens to all my ideas and supports me unconditionally.

Many thanks to my early readers for their thoughtful comments and excellent catches and for taking the time to do so.

And finally, a shout-out to my readers for continuing to read, search, learn and never give up trying to live your best. You are the reason I continue to write. Your support and reviews keep me going. From the bottom of my heart and soul, thank you.

Connect with Wendi

My website:

https://www.healingforwardwithwendi.com/

Twitter:

https://twitter.com/LindenmuthWendi

Please leave a review of my book after reading it on Amazon, Goodreads, and Barnes & Noble.

Thank you!

Notes

www.ingramcontent.com/pod-product-compliance
Lightning Source LLC
Chambersburg PA
CBHW071359290426
44108CB00014B/1620